THE SHARING (

Stories about First Nations C

Text: Theresa Meuse-Dallien   Illustrations: Arthur Stevens

NIMBUS
PUBLISHING

Nimbus Publishing Limited
PO Box 9166
Halifax, NS B3K 5M8
(902) 455-4286

Printed and bound in Canada
NB0560

National Library of Canada Cataloguing in Publication Data

The sharing circle : stories at [illegible] culture / Theresa Meuse ; illustra[illegible]ens.
ISBN 978-1-55109-450-2

1. Micmac Indians—Juvenile fiction. 2. Micmac Indians—Religion—Juvenile fiction. I. Stevens, Arthur II. Title.

PS8576.E887S52 2003 jC813'.6 C2003-905746-1

Nimbus Publishing acknowledges the financial support for its publishing activities from the Government of Canada through the Canada Book Fund (CBF) and the Canada Council for the Arts, and from the Province of Nova Scotia through Film & Creative Industries Nova Scotia. We are pleased to work in partnership with Film & Creative Industries Nova Scotia to develop and promote our creative industries for the benefit of all Nova Scotians.

CONTENTS

DEDICATION

The Sharing Circle is dedicated to the following
people: my children, Kerry, Tammy and Matthew,
and my husband, Kevin, for their love and
patience; my mom, who passed on the gift of
writing and taught me the important things in life;
my dad for giving me our Mi'kmaw heritage and
for creating crafts that encouraged me to learn;
my brothers, Frank, Steve, David, and my sister,
Rose—I am proud to be their sister; my
granddaughter Alex—may she always be proud of
her Mi'kmaw heritage; and the rest of my family,
relatives and friends for their continued support
and encouraging words. A special thanks to all the
Elders who humbly share their wisdom with us.
Most of all, this book is dedicated to the Creator,
who continually blesses me with gifts, talents, and
opportunities. We'lalin and lots of love!

A special thank you to the organizations that have
helped develop these stories: Eastern Woodland
Publishing (Truro); Solus Publishing (Cape Breton);
the National Council for the Arts; Nova Scotia
Department of Education, Mi'kmaq Division;
Department of Indian and Northern Affairs
(Amherst); First Nation and Inuit Health Branch
(Halifax); and Nova Scotia Mi'kmaq Forestry.

THE EAGLE FEATHER

One summer afternoon, Matthew and his dad went walking through the woods near their home. As they walked, Matthew's dad talked about the many plants and animals found in the woods and how they are used by First Nations people. He explained that some plants and trees are used for making crafts and herbal medicines, and that animals can be used for food and clothing. All these things are a special part of First Nations culture.

Suddenly, Matthew spotted an eagle.
He stood very still to watch the great bird
soar in circles high above his head.
The eagle had a fish in his claws,
just caught from the brook.
Matthew was sure he was taking the fish
back to the nest to feed his family.
"That eagle sure is beautiful,"
whispered Matthew.
"Yes it is," replied his father.
"To see an eagle flying overhead is
a sign of good luck and happiness."
"Dad, tell me about the eagle again.
Why is it so important?" Matthew asked.
The story of the eagle was Matthew's favourite.
It seemed like every time he heard it
he learned something new.

Matthew's dad first heard
the story of the eagle from his own father.
"We believe that the eagle is
the most powerful bird in the sky, and
can fly higher than any other bird," he began.
"The eagle can also see for many miles,
which helps it search for food.
Of all the creatures on the earth,
the eagle can get the closest to heaven
and can help carry our prayers and messages
to the Creator. That is why eagle feathers
are important to First Nations people.
Not everyone has an eagle feather.
Normally, an eagle feather is given
to someone for a special reason.
It is one of the best gifts
that anyone can receive."

"Eagle feathers are used in many ways...
for example, drummers and dancers use
them during special ceremonies.
But I use mine when I say prayers.
I take the feather from
its special place and hold it
in my hands. When I finish,
I put the feather back
so that it doesn't
get lost or ruined."

The sun was starting to go down, so Matthew and his dad turned toward home. Matthew ran ahead, hoping to see the eagle just one more time. As Matthew searched the sky, his dad noticed an eagle feather lying on the ground. Before Matthew could see, he bent down, picked up the feather, and carefully slipped it under his jacket. When they arrived home, Matthew's mom came out to meet them. Matthew told her all about the walk in the woods and the eagle they saw.

Later, Matthew's dad showed her what he had found.
Matthew's mom took the eagle feather
and placed it on a piece of red and yellow silk.
She added some leather to the pointed end
of the feather and attached two
white beads to the leather pieces.
Then, together, Matthew's mom
and dad held the feather and
said a thank-you prayer to the Creator.
They were thankful for the feather,
which they wanted to give to Matthew
as a sign of their love.
When they were ready, they called
for Matthew. His mother held out
the feather and presented it to her son.
His eyes grew big and the smile
on his face showed his joy.
They told him how special he was
and that they loved him very much.
Matthew took the feather carefully,
promising to take good care
of it. He hugged them both
and ran off to his room.

Matthew was happy to
finally have his very own
eagle feather. It made him
feel special and it reminded
him of the woods,
his father and his mother,
and his culture.
Like his father, Matthew
found a special place
for his feather—a wooden
box where he kept
all his special gifts.

THE SHARING CIRCLE

THE SACRED HERBS

One day, Matthew's friend Jeremy came to play. The boys went to Matthew's room, which was filled with toys and games and books. It looked just like Jeremy's room, but a few things were different. Jeremy noticed a little box on the dresser. "What's this stuff in this little box?" Jeremy asked. "Those are sacred herbs," Matthew answered. "What are sacred herbs?" Jeremy wanted to know. Matthew put down the truck he was playing with and tried to think of how to explain the sacred herbs.

"In my culture, our ancestors used sacred herbs for many different things. Before cutting down a tree, they would sprinkle sacred herbs on the ground by the tree to show they were thankful to the Creator for providing the tree to use in their community. They used the wood from the tree to make fires so they could cook their food. They also used it for making tools and for building their wigwams or homes.

Our ancestors could make medicine from certain types of trees, which helped to cure illness or to keep people healthy. There were many things to say thank-you for and offerings were made every day. Parents still teach children why sacred herbs are important. My parents taught me, and showed me how to use them," said Matthew.

Matthew let Jeremy smell the herbs. Jeremy took a sniff and was amazed. "That smells great!" Jeremy said. Matthew smiled and explained that there were four special herbs inside the box: sweet grass, cedar, sage, and tobacco.

"My mom collected these herbs and put them in this box for whenever I want to use them," said Matthew. "Sometimes, when I am away from home, I carry some herbs in a pouch just in case I want to make an offering. To make an offering I sprinkle some herbs in a special place, usually outside, and then I say a prayer."

"Sometimes people burn the herbs in a special bowl or shell. The burning herbs create a smoke, and because the smoke goes in all directions, it helps take their prayers to the Creator. The smoke can also be used as a way to clean the body. Using our hands, we move the smoke toward different parts of our bodies. We believe that the smoke helps us think good thoughts. It helps our eyes to see the good things in the world and in people. It helps our mouths to speak only good words. It helps our feet to walk only on good paths. The smoke helps our hearts to feel happiness and love. When people burn herbs like this, it's called a smudging ceremony."

"So, the sacred herbs are very important," Jeremy said. "Yes they are," Matthew replied. "And as long as people are respectful, anyone can use sacred herbs for the same reasons we use them." Jeremy was excited to go home and tell his parents the things he had learned about Matthew's culture. But first, he had one more question for his friend: "Matthew, do you think your mother would give me some sacred herbs?" he asked. "Probably," said Matthew. "Let's go ask her."

And guess what? Matthew's mom said Yes!

THE SHARING CIRCLE
14

THE MEDICINE POUCH

Every year Matthew's family goes on a camping trip. They always camp in the same spot, and they always have a lot of fun. They hike on the trails, ride their bikes, swim in the lake, and cook food over a campfire.

One day, Matthew's father told him that the family was going camping the next day. There wasn't much time to pack, so Matthew made a list of everything he would need. Just as he was finishing his list, Kerry, his older sister, asked if she could help him get ready. Matthew thought that was a good idea, and they began to gather up his camping gear.

Just when Matthew thought
they were finished, he suddenly
remembered one more thing:
his medicine pouch. He ran
to his room to get it from
its secret hiding place.
The pouch was a gift from
his grandfather, who had made
it especially for Matthew.
His grandfather had explained
that this pouch was to be used
for holding things that are important
or sacred, things like sacred herbs
for making offerings,
special gifts, stones that
have a special meaning,
or anything else
that makes Matthew
feel happy.

"That is what owning a medicine pouch is all about…carrying things that have special meaning," Matthew's grandfather had said. Whenever Matthew touches or looks at the things in his medicine pouch, he feels happy. That is why these objects are known as "good medicines." Matthew's secret hiding place was his closet. He hid the pouch in there because these special things belonged only to him. If someone found the pouch and opened it, all the objects in it would have to be replaced. That was the custom of his First Nations culture.

Everyone in Matthew's family had a medicine pouch, and he knew that it was an important part of his culture. He was happy that his grandfather gave him a pouch, and he filled it with special things right away. First, he put in some sacred herbs, just in case he wanted to say a prayer. He also carried a small, beautiful eagle feather that his mother and father had given him, and a stone that sparkled with many different colours.

When it was time to leave for the camping trip,
Matthew wore his medicine pouch around his neck.
It dangled like a necklace.
His sister attached her pouch to her belt.
Matthew's dad put his pouch in his pocket,
and his mom carried hers in her purse.
Now they were ready to go.

When Matthew's family arrived at the campsite, they set up their tent and unpacked all their camping gear. When that was finished, they decided to go for a walk. While they were hiking along the trail, they came upon the most beautiful bush Matthew had ever seen. Its leaves were all the colours of the rainbow, and it was as tall as he was.

"What kind of bush is this?"
Matthew asked his mother.
"I don't know," she said,
"but I hope this bush
will always be here
for others to see."

Matthew was quiet for a minute, then he opened his medicine pouch and took out his sacred herbs. The herbs were small pieces of sweet grass, cedar, tobacco, and sage. He gave each person in his family some of the herbs, which they sprinkled around the bush. As the herbs fell from their fingers to the earth, they said a prayer, asking the Creator to protect this bush and keep it beautiful. When Matthew and his family walked away from the bush, they all hoped it would be there next year, when they came back.

Each year after that, Matthew and his family
returned to the same campground,
and each year the bush was there
beside the trail. But one summer,
there was a big surprise
waiting for them.
Instead of one bush,
there were two!
A tiny sapling had
sprung up beside
the bigger bush.
Matthew was so happy
that he reached into
his medicine pouch for
some sacred herbs.
As he sprinkled them
on the ground, he
wished for more of
these beautiful
bushes every year.

THE DREAM CATCHER

Matthew and Dustin were good friends. It was Dustin's birthday, and many children were invited to his party. Matthew's dad had made Dustin a very special present. Matthew hoped Dustin would like it.

Matthew was the first to arrive at Dustin's house, and he carefully placed his present on the table. When the other children arrived, they all went outside to play. Dustin's father and grandmother stayed inside to prepare food for the party.

Outside, Dustin and Matthew played in the sandbox.
"I hope you like the present I brought you," said Matthew.
"My dad made it just for you."
Dustin smiled at Matthew, then sighed.
"I hope it will help me have good dreams.
Sometimes I have bad dreams and
I don't like them."
Matthew stopped playing.
"Did someone tell you what my present is, Dustin?"
he asked.
"No," answered Dustin. "Why?"
"Oh, just wondering…" Matthew said,
shrugging his shoulders.
He was surprised
to hear Dustin say he
hoped the present would
help him have
good dreams, because
that was exactly
what his present
would do.

After playing, the children went inside to eat sandwiches
and birthday cake. When they finished eating,
Dustin began to open his presents. He was very excited,
quickly ripping the wrapping paper off each one.
He unwrapped a toy truck with red stripes,
a baseball and bat, a kite with yellow streamers,
a storybook, and many other wonderful gifts.

Finally, there was only one present left, the one Matthew had brought.
Dustin picked up the package and carefully unwrapped it.
Finally, he held up the present for everyone to see.
Dustin was holding something he had never seen before,
something shaped in a circle and covered with leather.
The inside of the circle looked like a spider's web. In the web was a blue bead.
Dangling from the circle's edges were three fringes that held
more blue beads and beautiful blue feathers.

"Wow," said Dustin, touching one of the feathers. "What is this?"

"It's a dream catcher," said Matthew. "The dream catcher has been used for a long time to help people have good dreams. Some people use it just for decoration, but I gave you this dream catcher so you will have good dreams." Just then, Dustin remembered playing in the sandbox and talking about a present that would help him have good dreams. Now he knew why Matthew had looked so surprised.

Soon it was time for everyone to go home.
Dustin thanked all his friends for coming
to his party and for the presents they had
brought. When the children left,
Dustin ran to his bedroom and
hung the dream catcher above his bed.
That night, before going to sleep,
Dustin stared up at the
dream catcher hanging
on his wall.
"I sure hope this
dream catcher will
help me have good
dreams," he thought.
Then he said his prayers
and drifted off to sleep,
glad that Matthew
had given him
such a special gift.

THE SHARING CIRCLE
30

THE TALKING CIRCLE

 Matthew was on his way to attend the first Boy Scouts meeting. He was very excited because his uncle was a group leader. Matthew had never been to a Boy Scouts meeting before, but knowing his uncle would be at the meeting helped him to be less afraid. When Matthew arrived, he noticed there were a lot of boys.

Everyone was talking and laughing.

"Scouts is going to be fun," thought Matthew.

Soon Matthew's uncle and two other group leaders asked everyone to find a seat.

Boys scampered in all directions.

Some sat on the floor. Some sat in chairs by the wall, while others chose to sit by the window. One of the group leaders asked the boys to introduce themselves.

Everyone began talking all at once.

"What a lot of noise!" Matthew thought. He could barely hear himself think.

Finally, in a loud voice one of the leaders told everyone to be quiet.
He said that each boy should take a turn introducing himself.
One at a time, each boy shared stories about his family.
Some boys talked about their brothers and sisters.
Some lived with their dads while others lived with their grandparents.
Some talked about their pets and favourite toys.

When the last boy finished introducing himself, the leaders talked about rules as well as some of the activities the boys would get to do at future meetings. As the leaders talked, they walked around the room, turning their heads so they could see all the boys. Matthew was having problems hearing the leaders, so he raised his hand to tell them. The other boys agreed that they could not hear very well either.

"What are we going to do?" asked the group leaders.

Matthew's uncle smiled and told the other two leaders that he had an idea that just might work. He asked the class if they wanted to learn about his First Nations culture. The boys raised their hands or nodded in agreement. Matthew's uncle explained that, in his culture, when a lot of people gather to talk, they do it in a special way. First, everyone sits in a circle. Then a leader is chosen. The leader is responsible for making sure that everyone gets a chance to talk, and everyone else must listen. The leader does this by using a talking stick.

When a person holds a talking stick, it is their turn to talk. If they do not wish to say anything, they pass the stick to the next person. Matthew's uncle explained that he had been a leader in many talking circles, and that some leaders might choose to use something other than a stick, like a small stone or a feather. For their talking circle, Matthew's uncle chose a beautiful stone that fit perfectly in the palm of his hand. After asking everyone to form a circle, he introduced himself. When he had finished, he passed the stone to the boy on his left.

The talking stick is always passed in the same direction that the hands of a clock move. Each boy took a turn, and everyone was able to hear easily. When they had all had a turn, Matthew's uncle explained that when everyone sits in a circle, it's easy to see each other and to hear each other's voices. In the circle, everyone is treated as an equal. The circle also teaches people to have respect for others. No one is allowed to talk or disturb the person who is talking. People learn how to listen and be patient because they have to wait their turn. They also learn to have a good memory because if someone wants to respond to something that someone else has said, they must remember the idea until it is their turn to talk. "So the talking circle is very useful and teaches people a lot of things," said Matthew's uncle.

The boys thanked Matthew's uncle for teaching them about the talking circle. Just before leaving the circle, one boy raised his hand and asked if they could start each meeting with a talking circle.

The group leaders smiled at each other and decided that would be a great idea. From that day on, whenever the Boy Scouts had their meetings, they all gathered in a talking circle.

Best of all, the boys took turns choosing the talking stick for each meeting—they liked that idea best!

THE MEDICINE WHEEL

Every year, Matthew's dad brings Matthew and his brother Josh to the doctor for a checkup, just to make sure they stay healthy. The boys don't mind going. Their doctor is a Mi'kmaq who grew up in their community. When Matthew and Josh arrive at the doctor's office, they sit in chairs next to the aquarium. They love to watch the fish swimming back and forth. There are always interesting things to look at in the doctor's waiting room, and many good books to read.

Matthew and Josh especially like the pictures on the walls. A poster on one wall shows healthy food, like fruits and vegetables. On another wall is a picture of trees in a circle around a lake, and on another, a picture of someone praying. On his last visit, after looking at the picture on the fourth wall—a happy-looking family eating popcorn by a fireplace—Matthew exclaimed, "It's like the medicine wheel. The picture of the woman in church is hanging in the east, and the picture of the trees around the lake is in the south. The picture of the family sitting together is in the north..."

"...and the picture of the good food is in the west," Josh added.

Their dad was pleased that his sons remembered the story he had told them about the medicine wheel.

"Do you know what each picture stands for?" he asked. Matthew answered right away.

"The picture in the east is for spirituality. It tells us to believe in the Creator and respect all things that are given to us."

"The picture from the south," replied Josh, "is for the environment—so we

don't forget to respect the earth and to make sure we don't destroy all the trees and water. The picture of the good food, in the west, is for our health. That means we should eat good food, exercise, and get enough sleep."

"What about the picture in the north, Matthew?" his dad asked.
Matthew thought for a moment. "That's all about good mental
health," he answered. "It means we should always try to stay healthy
in our minds, even when things happen that make us sad or angry.
The people in the picture look happy, don't they dad?"
Matthew's father nodded his head,
proud of his sons for knowing so much
about the medicine wheel.

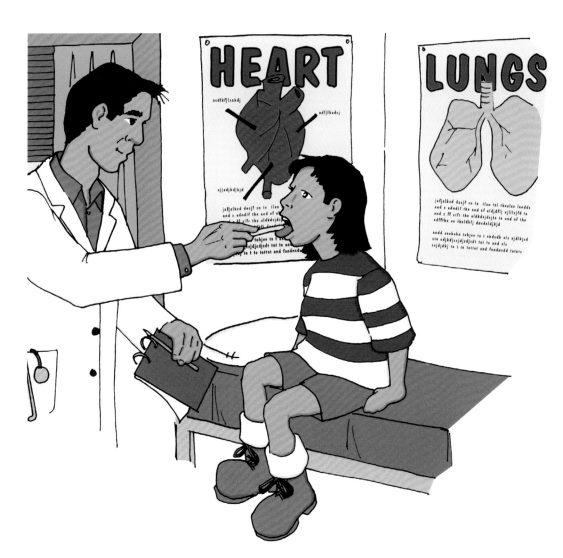

Just then, the nurse called their names and the boys went into the doctor's office. The doctor asked them how they were feeling and he checked their eyes, nose, and throat. Then he listened to their hearts with his stethoscope, and looked into their ears with his little light. Afterwards, he made some notes, and told Matthew and Josh that they were in good health. Matthew looked at his dad. "I guess coming to the doctor for a checkup is just one more way to be healthy."

The doctor smiled. "You boys must know about the medicine wheel."
Matthew and Josh grinned and nodded.
The doctor pointed to the medicine wheel hanging on his office wall. In the middle of the circle, strips of leather lay in the four directions. Leather fringes hung from the circle, and feathers and beads dangled from each fringe. "The medicine wheel is a reminder of the teachings of our culture," he said.
"Every day it reminds me how important it is to do things to stay healthy. Many First Nations people believe the medicine wheel helps people understand how to live life on earth as best as they can."

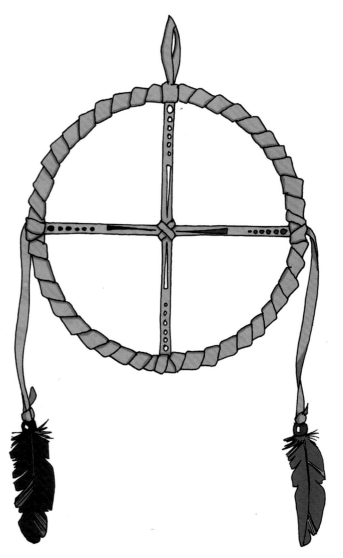

On the way home, they decided they wanted to make their own medicine wheels. Their dad found some scraps of leather, feathers and beads for them to use. When the medicine wheels were finished, the boys hung them in their rooms. It felt so good to have a medicine wheel that they decided to make some more to give to their best friends at school.

THE SHARING CIRCLE
44

THE DRUM

Today was an exciting day for Matthew. His teacher had chosen him to be the one to bring something from home for Show and Tell. After school, Matthew ran home to tell his mom and sister the good news.

His sister Tammy was almost as excited as he was.

"What are you going to take?" she asked.

Matthew thought for a moment. "I think I'll take my drum and play it for the class."

"That sounds like a good idea," said his mother.

"Tammy," asked Matthew, "would you come to school with me? We can play the drums and sing some songs together."

Over the next few days, Matthew and Tammy practised their songs so they would not make any mistakes when the big day came. Finally Show and Tell day arrived. When Matthew and Tammy came into the classroom, the teacher introduced Tammy to the students and explained that Matthew and Tammy were going to share their First Nations culture with them. She told the class that they were going to hear some traditional drumming and singing.

Matthew and Tammy picked up their drums and drumsticks, and began tapping a steady rhythm. Bom, bom, bom, bom, sounded the drums, as Matthew and Tammy began to sing their first song.
They had chosen "The Honour Song" as a way of saying thank you to the class for allowing them to play their drums and sing.

When they finished, the room echoed with clapping and cheering. This made Matthew and Tammy proud and happy —the children liked their performance!

After singing another song, "The Feast Song," Matthew and Tammy asked students if they had any questions. "How do you make that drum?" asked one girl. Matthew explained that a hand drum is made from deer or moose hide. The hide is tanned into leather and stretched over special wood and tied along the edges with rawhide or other strong material. "The drum is then dried for several days before it is played" said Matthew, "To give the drum a better sound, it is usually heated."

Another boy raised his hand. "Are there other kinds of drums?"
"Yes," Tammy answered, "there is also a large, round drum
that many people can play at one time. The round drum is
usually played at special gatherings by a group of drummers
and singers who practice every day. At gatherings, many people
like to dance. Since the large drum can be very loud,
it is a good drum for dancing."

"What kind of dancing do the people do?" asked another boy.
"It's not modern dancing," explained Tammy, "but special dances that are part of First Nations culture."

Matthew's teacher asked if there were any other important things that the class should know about the drum.

"Many First Nations people believe that the beat of the drum is like the heartbeat of Mother Earth. When prayers are said during drumming, the beat helps send messages and prayers to God," Matthew said.

"So is the drum a sacred object?" asked the teacher.

"Yes," said Tammy, "and so we should show respect at all times—not only to the drum, but to the drummers as well."

THE DRUM

The teacher asked Matthew and Tammy if they would teach the class a song. "That would be easy," Matthew said. He asked the children to form a large circle, then he and Tammy taught them the words to "The Gathering Song." "This song is usually played at special gatherings like powwows and other celebrations in the community," said Tammy. Soon everyone was singing to the steady beat of drums. When the song ended, the teacher thanked Matthew and Tammy for bringing the drums and for singing their songs. On their way home from school, Matthew and Tammy talked about how much fun it was to share their culture with the other children.